Comparing Past and Present

Taking a Trip

Rebecca Rissman

Heinemann
LIBRARY

Chicago, Illinois

© 2014 Heinemann Library
an imprint of Capstone Global Library, LLC
Chicago, Illinois

To contact Capstone Global Library please phone 800-747-4992, or visit our website www.capstonepub.com

Edited by Rebecca Rissman, Daniel Nunn, and Catherine Veitch
Designed by Philippa Jenkins
Picture research by Elizabeth Alexander
Production by Helen McCreath
Originated by Capstone Global Library Ltd
Printed and bound in China

17 16 15 14 13
10 9 8 7 6 5 4 3 2 1

Library of Congress Cataloging-in-Publication Data
Rissman, Rebecca.
 Taking a trip / Rebecca Rissman.
     pages cm.—(Comparing past and present)
 Includes bibliographical references and index.
 ISBN 978-1-4329-8994-1 (hb)—ISBN 978-1-4329-9028-2 (pb) 1.
Travel—History—Juvenile literature. I. Title.
 G175.R58 2014
 910.4—dc23   2013012547

Acknowledgments
We would like to thank the following for permission to reproduce photographs: © Capstone Publishers p. 5 (Karon Dubke); Alamy pp. 6 (© ClassicStock), 12 (© Vintage Images), 13 (© Juice Images), 20 (© Archive Pics), 22 (© INTERFOTO); Corbis pp. 4 (© H. Armstrong Roberts), 15 (© Redlink Production), 23 (© Redlink Production); Getty Images pp. 8 (Hulton Archive/Topical Press Agency), 18 (Hulton Archive/Sasha), 21 (Gallo Images/Danita Delimont); Shutterstock pp. 7 (© Pavel L Photo and Video), 11 (© cynoclub), 17 (© Pavel L Photo and Video); SuperStock pp. 9 (Alex Mares-Manton/Asia Images), 10, 14, 16 (Universal Images Group), 19, 23.

Front cover photographs of a young couple enjoying a car ride, 1907, reproduced with permission of Superstock (Everett Collection), and a family loading inflatables into a car reproduced with permission of Getty Images (Image Source). Back cover photograph of people in a horse-drawn carriage, New Hampshire, reproduced with permission of Superstock.

We would like to thank Nancy Harris and Diana Bentley for their invaluable help in the preparation of this book.

Every effort has been made to contact copyright holders of material reproduced in this book. Any omissions will be rectified in subsequent printings if notice is given to the publisher.

Contents

Comparing the Past and Present

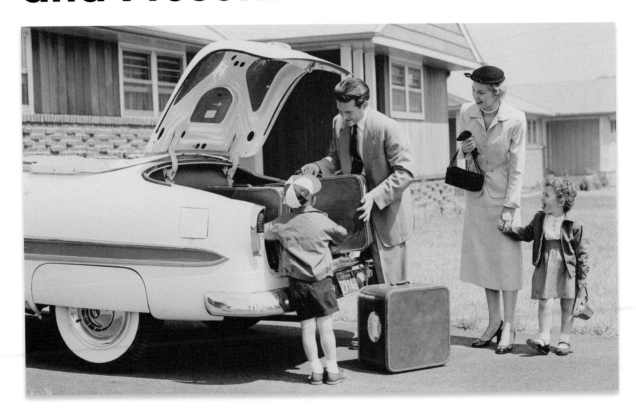

Things in the past have already happened.

Things in the present are happening now.

Traveling has changed over time.

The way people take trips today is very different from in the past.

Getting Around

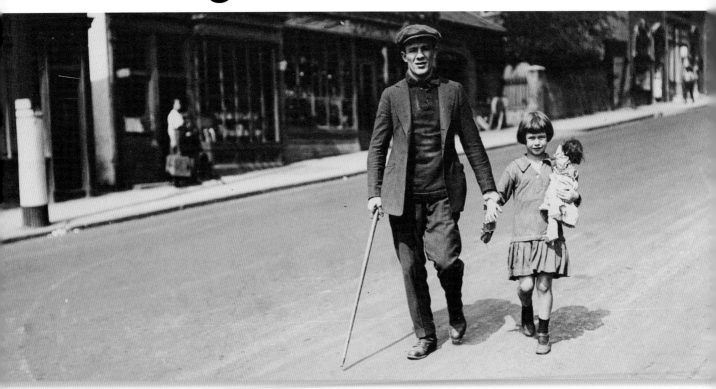

In the past, most people walked from place to place.

Today, many people only walk
a short way.

In the past, many people used horses to travel.

Today, some people ride horses for fun.

In the past, few people took trips in cars.

Today, many people take trips in cars.

In the past, people traveled across oceans in large ships.

Today, people can travel across oceans in airplanes.

Who Travels?

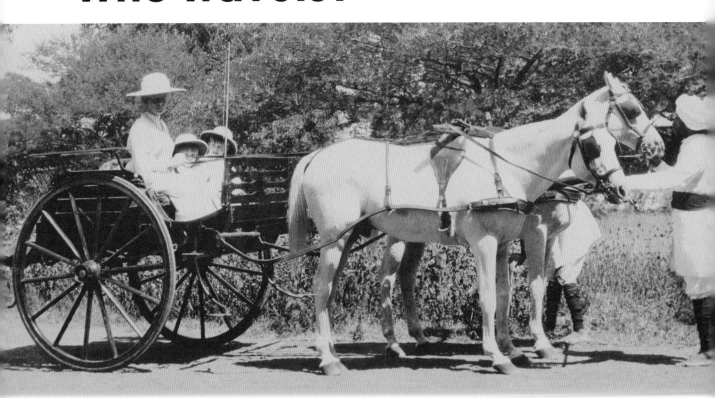

In the past, only rich families went on long trips.

Today, many families go on
long trips.

How Long Did It Take?

In the past, it could take weeks to
travel to a new place.

Today, people can travel around the world in just hours.

Why Travel?

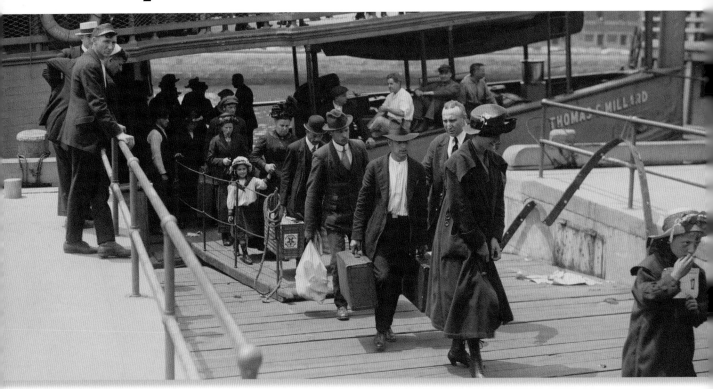

In the past, some people traveled far away to start a new life.

Today, people also travel for work and to see new places.

Then and Now

In the past, people went on trips for fun.
Today, people still go on trips for fun!

Picture Glossary

 airplane large machine that flies through the air

 ship large boat that carries many people a long way

Index

Note to Parents and Teachers

Before reading

Talk to children about the difference between the past and present. Explain that things that have already happened are in the past. Remind children of a classroom activity that took place a day or two ago, and explain how that activity happened in the past. Then explain that the conversation you are having now is in the present.

After reading

- Explain to children that the way people travel has changed over time. Ask children to think of different modes of transportation, such as car, bicycle, airplane, or train. Then explain that some of these modes of transportation did not exist in the past.

- Tell children that the word *vacation* means a special trip people take to enjoy themselves. Ask children if they have ever taken a vacation. If so, ask them to explain where they went, how they got there, and how long the trip took. Then, as a group, brainstorm about how the trip might have been different if it had taken place in the past.

- Ask children if they have ever seen or ridden a horse. Explain that in the past, many people used horses for transportation. Show children the photo on page 10. Ask if they think traveling by horse would have been fast or slow.